GRAND CANYON

and

The National Parks of Arizona and Utah

GALLERY BOOKS
An Imprint of W. H. Smith Publishers Inc.
112 Madison Avenue
New York City 10016

This edition first published in U.S.
in 1991 by Gallery Books,
an imprint of W.H. Smith Publishers, Inc.
112 Madison Avenue, New York, New York 10016

ISBN 0-8317-0257-5

Printed and bound in Spain

For rights information about the photographs in
this book please contact:

The Image Bank
111 Fifth Avenue, New York, NY 10003

Producer: Solomon M. Skolnick
Writer: Erin Hennessey
Design Concept: Lesley Ehlers
Designer: Ann-Louise Lipman
Editor: Sara Colacurto
Production: Valerie Zars
Photo Researcher: Edward Douglas
Assistant Photo Researcher: Robert V. Hale
Editorial Assistant: Carol Raguso

Title page: *The shifting light of day
changes the color and appearance of
rock formations in the Grand Canyon
National Park.* Opposite: *The Grand
Canyon's geological history, repre-
senting some two billion years of the
earth's development, can be seen in its
layers of exposed earth and rock.*

Miles and miles of uninterrupted land make up much of the American Southwest. Here, free from the hustle of the city, the scale is so large that skyscrapers would virtually disappear if tossed inside the vast gorges of the Grand Canyon. Statues that appear majestic in city squares would look like mere toys if placed next to the immense rock formations of Bryce Canyon and Zion National Park.

The diverse landscape of the Southwest includes grassy plains, mountains, plateaus, river valleys, and a variety of deserts. But the canyon country of Arizona and southern Utah has, by far, some of the most extraordinary scenery in the entire world.

Of all the impressive sights in this part of the country, the Grand Canyon is easily the most remarkable. Officially designated as one of the seven natural wonders of the world, this giant of all canyons ranges from one-half to 18 miles wide. The distance around the canyon from the North Rim to the South Rim amounts to 215 miles; the vertical drop from the canyon's rim to its floor is about one mile. The Colorado River – the primary sculptor of the land for more than six million years – flows along the canyon floor. Moving at an average speed of four miles per hour, this mighty river flows west through the canyon, later turning south to eventually empty into the Gulf of California in Mexico.

Surrounding the Grand Canyon is the 1,000-square-mile Grand Canyon National Park. This kingdom includes portions of the Conconino and Kaibab Plateaus, which are crowned by handsome forests. The park is also home to an Indian village—the ancestral home of the Havasupais—as well as some 300 prehistoric ruins.

Visitors approaching the Grand Canyon must ascend more than 7,000 feet to reach the rim. As the elevation increases, the climate changes, and so does the landscape: The road to the top passes through grasslands and sagebrush flats before reaching an array of juniper trees, pinyon, and ponderosa pine.

From the rim, visitors can see the tops of mountains that measure 2,000 feet or more from their bases within the canyon. This first glimpse of the Grand Canyon is awesome. People often react by speaking in hushed tones as if they are in a place of worship. Overwhelmed by the canyon's enormity and powerful presence, some even cry.

Native American tribes have long treated the canyon with spiritual reverence. In the Hopi religion, it is believed that the Grand Canyon is the place where

Passing clouds cast shadows on the rocky cliffs of the Grand Canyon, enhancing its ever-changing face. Overleaf: A rich desert sunset washes over the Grand Canyon, creating a breathtaking view before darkness descends.

Above: *Sunrise on the North Rim of the Grand Canyon. Shades of gold, pink, and blue color the morning sky above the mist-covered canyon.* Left: *Erosion is partly responsible for the dramatic rock formations that make up the Grand Canyon. Ancient volcanic activity also played a role.* Opposite: *The mighty rock pedestals in Grand Canyon National Park are named for the gods of ancient myths. These awesome formations evoke powerful emotions in the park's many visitors.*

man first emerged from the underworld. The Hopis believe that the dead return to the village of Sipapu – the entrance to the underworld – located in the canyon of the Little Colorado River about five miles from that river's junction with the Colorado River. For centuries it has been the destination of pilgrimages by the Hopi tribe.

Clarence E. Dutton, a prominent geologist who wrote the first definitive scientific report on the canyon more than a century ago, was also struck by the spiritual quality of the canyon. His response was to name its many buttes and other rock formations after sacred temples in India, China, and Egypt, such as the Brahma Temple, Buddha Temple, and the Osiris Temple.

Adding to the Grand Canyon's mystical allure is the fact that it is constantly changing. Day after day, its walls widen and reshape themselves due to erosion caused by the river, the weather, and the four million tourists who walk its trails each year.

Its appearance also changes with the time of day. A spectacular occurrence at the canyon is the sunrise over its eastern ridge. The view is reminiscent of a picture of the earth taken from space – half of the earth is bathed in light and the other half is covered in darkness. The canyon eventually becomes completely visible although much of it remains in the shadows until the sun directly hits particular stretches of land. As the sun moves, the canyon's colors shift, with the shadowy areas often appearing blue and pink and the illuminated areas taking on a rich orange and gold tone.

For years, painters have been coming to the Grand Canyon to capture these beautiful colors on canvas. One of the most famous is the nineteenth-century landscape artist Thomas Moran whose painting *The Grand Chasm of the Colorado* hangs in the United States Capitol building. The Grand Canyon's Moran Point, a vista point of 7,157 feet, was named for the painter.

Moran's painting was one of the things that first brought public attention to the canyon. As the Southwest was developed by farmers, miners, and ranchers, the Grand Canyon and its surrounding land was exploited. Pressured by early environmentalists, President Benjamin Harris managed to establish the canyon as a forest reserve in 1893, thereby protecting it from homesteaders, miners, and others in commercial pursuit. More than a decade passed before President Theodore Roosevelt declared the area a game preserve to protect the animals; later he designated it a national monument under the terms of a new law, which placed a ban on prospecting and mining for minerals.

The Grand Canyon's Vermilion Cliffs glow in the early morning sun as the gorge below sits in darkness.

Left: *The beautiful banded cliffs within the Grand Canyon descend to the hot, dry environment of the canyon floor.* Below: *Few trees and shrubs can survive in the semiarid climate of the Grand Canyon. Those that do are hearty species that cling to the soil, providing food and shelter for some of the area's wildlife.* Opposite: *Hikers cross the natural bridge over Angel's Window in Grand Canyon National Park, as the Colorado River flows in the distance.*

In 1916, the National Park Service was established to create and administer the regulations that would preserve areas of great natural beauty. But it wasn't until 1919, that a bill was finally passed by both houses of Congress to establish the Grand Canyon National Park. Additional land was added in 1927, 1932, the late 1960's, and again in 1975, making Grand Canyon National Park a relative newcomer to the national park system. (Other parks, like Yosemite and Yellowstone, had been granted national park status in the late 1800's.)

Scientists also wanted to protect the Grand Canyon, but not just to preserve its natural splendor. Here scientists have a view of geological time that goes back at least two billion years. Perhaps nowhere on earth has such a geological record been so clearly exposed as within the stratified walls of the Grand Canyon.

Within the depths of the Grand Canyon lies the beginning of a grand sequence of rock layers. North of the Grand Canyon, in southwest Utah, Zion Canyon's giant amber-colored rocks represent the earth's middle geological history. A more recent chapter can be found even farther north in the rock strata of Utah's Bryce Canyon National Park.

Below: *At nearly 1,800 miles long, the Colorado River is one of America's longest.* Opposite, top: *Metamorphic and sedimentary rock make up most of the Grand Canyon's primordial landscape. The Colorado River continuously shapes the canyon by eroding its soil and rock.* Bottom: *Deep in the Grand Canyon, the muddy Colorado flows red with sediment as it winds its way past some of the world's oldest exposed rock.*

The terrain of southern Utah further exemplifies this geological layering. The rising "stairs" in the Grand Staircase from the Grand Canyon to Bryce, consist of a series of cliffs formed by different types of rock from different periods of the earth's past. The south-facing cliffs are named for their prominent colors: The "stair" nearest the Utah-Arizona border has a red-brown hue; hence, this stretch of cliffs is known as the Chocolate Cliffs. The rock here is more than 200 million years old. Climbing northward, the Vermilion Cliffs are a deeper red than their chocolate neighbors. In contrast to these rich colored bluffs are the White Cliffs, which are composed of sandstone; the Grey Cliffs, of a lighter sandstone; and the final stair, the Pink Cliffs of Bryce Canyon, which contain the youngest rock in the staircase.

In addition to geology, the Grand Canyon tells an interesting story about the southwest region's flora and fauna. Although the canyon's North Rim and South Rim are only about nine miles apart, they are really quite different. The North Rim is about 1,200 feet higher than the South Rim and is similar to Canada in climate and vegetation. The South Rim, by contrast, is more arid, receiving half as much snow and rain than its northern counterpart. There are certain plants and animals on one side of the canyon that, because of distinct differences in elevation and climate, are either

The Grand Canyon is the largest canyon in North America. It is known as the "Big Ditch" by natives of Arizona.

Preceding page: *A raft navigates a mild stretch of the Colorado. Downriver lies a more challenging course.* This page, above: *Mather Point on the Grand Canyon's South Rim, named after the National Park Service's first director, Steve Mather, is the first stop for most of the park's visitors. Its rounded rock formations provide a dramatic contrast to the more jagged peaks found along the canyon's rim.* Below: *From Mather Point, where guardrails protect observers from a sheer drop, a mere fourth of the Grand Canyon is visible.*

absent or have evolved differently on the other. Together the North and South Rims are home to 70 species of mammals, including the mule deer, tassel-eared squirrel, bobcat, mountain lion, and coyote. In addition, there are 250 species of birds, 30 species of reptiles and amphibians, 26 species of fish, and 1,500 species of plants.

The more popular South Rim is open to visitors year-round. The North Rim is much quieter, with severe winters that typically shut this side of the park down from November to May. It is difficult to visit both rims on the same trip, for, although the rims are under 10 miles apart as the crow flies, one must drive the 215 miles around the eastern end of the canyon to get from one rim to the other.

Because of its size and changes in elevation, the climate, landscape, and wildlife *within* the Grand Canyon also vary greatly. In general, hiking from the floor of the canyon to the uppermost point of the South Rim is like passing from the hot, dry Mexican border to the cooler climes of Canada.

The different seasons, however, bring temperature fluctuations. In winter, for example, the canyon floor stays relatively warm, usually in the mid- to low 60's, while high above, the ground is sometimes covered in snow with temperatures well below freezing. During the summer, the temperature on the canyon floor can climb to over 100 degrees Fahrenheit, while temperatures on the rims hover in the high 70's, depending on the wind.

Preceding page: *The ragged edge of the South Rim offers superb views of the canyon's terrain.* This page, right: *Located on the edge of the South Rim, the Desert View Watchtower, designed by Mary Jane Colter, was built in 1933 in the ancient pueblo style. Its winding staircase leads to an observation deck.* Below: *The Watchtower's ceiling reveals a pattern found in Native American ceremonial chambers.* Following pages, left: *Along the West Rim of the Grand Canyon is Powell Memorial, named in honor of John Wesley Powell, the great explorer of the Grand Canyon and the Colorado River.* Right: *Vegetation clings to the eroding soil of the hard and soft rock of the Grand Canyon, adding to its variety of colors.*

Afternoon rain showers are also common in the summer, with lightning often ushering in the storms.

While the Grand Canyon stands alone by virtue of its size and splendor, there are other gorges in the Southwest that are also extraordinary in their own right. Each one has a distinctive look, shaped over time by eroding forces that continue to pare layers of rock down to uncommon shapes, colors, and sizes.

Arches National Park, established only in 1971, is a good example of just how un-usual natural rock formations can really get. Located in the red-rock country of southeastern Utah, this relatively small reserve is home to a dramatic collection of natural stone arches, windows, spires, and pinnacles. Some are so thin and delicate that it's a wonder they're still standing. Others, like the Parade of Elephants and the Three Gossips, have such a strong resemblance to animals and humans that it's hard to believe that they haven't been carved by human hands.

The forces that shape the sandstone of Arches National Park include snow, ice, wind, and water. The erosion is gradual yet continuous and several of the monumental structures appear

During the winter months an added serenity graces the Grand Canyon as snow falls along its rims. The North Rim receives about 140 inches of snow annually, while the South Rim only receives about 60.

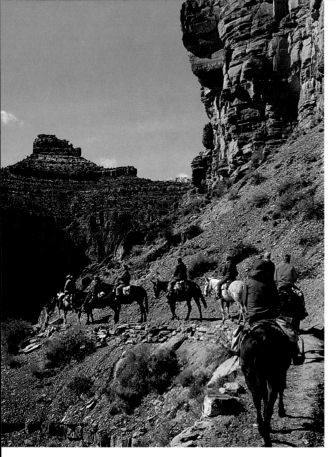
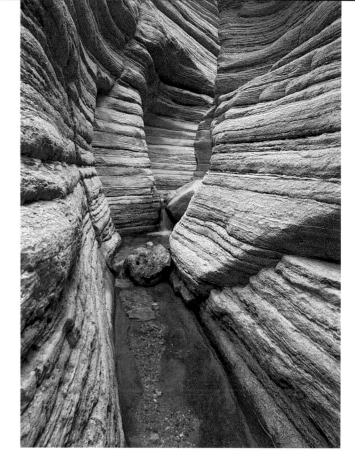

Above, left: *Mules have carried visitors and their provisions up and down the precarious trails of the Grand Canyon for decades.*
Right: *Matkatamiba Canyon is one of several "smaller" canyons within the Grand Canyon. Here, a narrow stream flows between two walls of striated rock.* Below: *Deep within the Grand Canyon, the towering, burnished walls of limestone in Marble Gorge create an awesome spectacle.* Opposite: *The Grand Canyon Railway, originally commissioned into service in 1901, has been reintroduced to transport visitors across Arizona's northern plains and Kaibab National Forest to the Canyon's South Rim.*

ripe for a change. Landscape Arch, at 291 feet across, 106 feet high, and in one section only six feet thick, exemplifies these engineering anomalies. To be sure, the delicate span of arch will one day give in to time and gravity, but for now it (and the park's other arches) continues to delight Arches' many visitors.

Just south of Arches is Canyonlands, which was established as a national park in 1964. Named for its more than 100 miles of canyons, broad mesas, towering spires, and the roaring rapids of the Colorado River and its tributaries all contribute to this park's stunning variety of form and color. Abandoned villages with ancient drawings can also be found here, indicating that humans have inhabited these desert rocks, off and on, for thousands of years.

At the center of Canyonlands, the Green River pours into the Colorado. The Confluence, as this meeting point is known, forms a Y-shaped gorge that divides the park into three sections. The Island in the Sky mesa to the north, the Maze to the west, and the Needles district to the south and east are all distinct in their landscapes, but each offers superb views of the park's natural wonders.

The Maze, or the Land of Standing Rocks (as it was called by early Native Americans), has perhaps the most primitive quality of all. Here, a confusing

The Courthouse Towers in Utah's Arches National Park are an example of the weird and wonderful shapes into which the sandstone has eroded.

Above, left to right: *Balanced Rock in Arches National Park stands precariously atop its narrow pedestal. This arch, appropriately named Delicate Arch, is one of the many spectacular arches from which Arches National Park derives its name.* Below: *Landscape Arch defies the laws of gravity.*

Right: *Right now, Double "O" Arch reveals a symmetry that looks almost too perfect to be an act of nature. Eventually erosion will attack that symmetry, causing the rock to take on a new formation.* Below: *Like tree roots reaching for water, Double Arch, one of 64 arches in Arches' Devil's Garden, delicately extends between two rock formations.*

Below: *A towerlike structure stands adjacent to the curved rock of Turret Arch in Arches National Park.* Opposite: *The Windows sit among scrub brush and sand in Arches' red-rock region in southeastern Utah.*

labyrinth of sheer canyons sur-
rounds towering fins of stone and
enormous buttes. The animals
that flourish in the Maze—
kangaroo rats, coyotes, lizards—
are highly adapted to the district's extreme climate: In
summer, temperatures soar to
120 degrees Fahrenheit, and in
winter, they drop to as low as
−20 degrees.

Due west of Canyonlands
is Capitol Reef, designated a
national park in 1971. The "reef"
in this case refers to a ridge of
rock made up of deeply colored
bands of sandstone and shale.
Capitol Dome, rising a thousand
feet above the Fremont River,
marks one of the canyon's high
points. This particular rock formation bears some resemblance
to the dome of the U.S. Capitol
building, although some would
say that Washington, D.C.'s man-
made structure doesn't come
close to matching the golden
majesty of this natural wonder.

Capitol Reef harbors two
distinct landscapes: the lush
growth along the banks of the
Fremont River and the barren
rock of the stone cliffs. Like
Canyonlands, the plants and
animals that flourish here are
remarkably adapted to the
rigorous climate and rugged
terrain. Some plants survive by
growing near the park's rare
streams and waterholes, and, of
course, the Fremont; others have
long or spreading root systems
that allow them to reach deep for
groundwater; still others survive,
ironically, by having a very short
lifespan, leaving seeds behind to
grow when the conditions are
just right. Many of the animals
have adapted by becoming night
creatures, rarely leaving their
dens and burrows during the
brutal daylight hours. A surpris-
ing array of wildlife, including

The Colorado River and its tributaries are the primary sculptors of the canyons in Utah's Canyonlands National Park.

Above: *Arches are also present in Canyonlands, as demonstrated by this arch in the making.* Left: *This broad, red-rock formation, rising from Davis Canyon, is part of more than 100 miles of canyons in Canyonlands National Park.* Opposite, top: *About 300 million years ago, an ancient sea covered Canyonlands. Today the park is a seemingly barren desert that receives less than 10 inches of rain a year.* Bottom: *Petroglyphs and pictographs reveal that humans have been living in this region since ancient times.*

Preceding page: *Angel Arch's The Molar is a good example of Canyonland's gravity-defying structures, as well as one of its strangest natural phenomena. Below: Canyonlands' Mesa Arch spans a body of jagged rocks on its cliffside perch. In the distance lie the La Sal Mountains.*

shrimp and toads, exists in the pockets of rainwater that often remain in the folds of the rock.

South of Capitol Reef is the high section of the Colorado Plateau. Here, Bryce Canyon National Park sits 7,000 to 9,000 feet above sea level—an altitude that some visitors may need to adjust to due to the thinness of the air at these heights.

Bryce Canyon was designated a national park in 1928 and was named after Ebenezer Bryce, an early homesteader (1875) who described the canyon as "a heck of a place to lose a cow." The odd-shaped, pink rock formations—hoodoos—that dot Bryce's eerie landscape are an accumulation of sand, silt, and lime. About 70 million years ago, sediments were pushed together and lifted up by powerful pressures within the earth, and over time erosion shaped the Pope, the Chinese Wall, and the many other freestanding forms found in the park.

An interesting contrast to the rugged canyon terrain of the park is the forest atop nearby Paunsaugunt Plateau. Fir, spruce, and silver-backed aspen seem starkly out of place in southern Utah, but they add wonderful smells, colors, and variety to Bryce.

The Egyptian Temple in south central Utah's Capitol Reef National Park rises majestically from its rocky base. Bands of color reveal layers of sandstone and shale.

Above: *Surrounding Hickman Bridge, a 133-foot natural bridge in Capitol Reef, are barren landscape and unusual rock formations that often resemble objects and animals.* Below: *A rising hill of gray stone is topped by a sheer white and brown rock formation in Capitol Reef National Park.* Opposite: *The cathedral-like Temple Of The Sun rises from Capitol Reef's desert floor.*

Zion National Park, in Utah's southwest corner, is a scenic area filled with sculptured stone. Located in a deep and majestic canyon, Zion is divided by the Virgin River, which cuts through both the White and Vermilion Cliffs. The river has been carving the canyon for millions of years and is responsible for the towering monoliths that form the canyon walls. Iron is the major cause of color in the canyon's red rocks; the iron has been leached over time from the white rocks.

The highest peak in Zion, which became a national park in 1919, is the West Temple whose sheer stone walls shoot up to 7,795 feet. One of the park's most notable features is the Great Arch—720 feet wide at the bottom and 580 feet high. All of the arches in this area, including Zion's Great Arch, are safe to pass under, as there appears to be little danger of the upper rocks falling.

Southeast of the Grand Canyon, near the New Mexico border, is another spectacle worth exploring: Arizona's Petrified Forest National Park, established in 1962, features thousands of fossilized trees, their structures preserved forever in brilliant crystals of quartz.

From Sunrise Point visitors are able to view a collection of colorful standing rocks scattered throughout Bryce Canyon.

Preceding page, above: *Bryce's
towering cliffs, pinnacles, and castles
(left) are known as hoodoos. They are
primarily the result of water erosion.
Delicate stone structures and massive
rock formations in brilliant colors and
subtle shades (right) illustrate the
diversity that exists within Bryce
Canyon. Below: Visitors can take
in the magnificent sight of Bryce
Amphitheater from Upper Inspiration
Point over Silent City. According to
Native American legend, the canyon
was created when a powerful animal
spirit turned all of its wicked followers
into stone, thus silencing them forever.
This page, above: Sparse vegetation
grows at the edge of a rocky cliff in
Bryce Canyon. The odd shaped stone
figures in the foreground take on an
almost magical quality in the afternoon sun. Right: The depths of Bryce
Canyon offer many dramatic views of
the bright sun hitting the red rocks
overhead.*

In Petrified Forest, hunks of agate and amethyst are scattered about where conifer trees once rested. The trees were originally carried down ancient streams and rivers to this point. When the giant trees came to rest, they were buried over time by sand, mud, and volcanic ash. The lack of oxygen beneath these layers preserved the trees, setting the stage for petrification. When the land shifted and rose with volcanic activity, the logs came to the surface, revealing the petrified wood that can be seen today.

Other fossils are also sprinkled throughout the park. Scientists are finding the petrified remains of crocodile-like phytosaurs, salamander-like metoposaurs, and heavily armored aetosaurs, as well as ancient seeds, cones, and fern fronds. These discoveries have helped explain some of the mysteries of the earth's past.

Zion National Park is huge in scale, consisting primarily of massive walls of sedimentary rock rising from deep within the canyon.

Topped by a thin layer of limestone, the West Temple is Zion's highest peak at 7,795 feet. Below: Unlike the red rocks covering most of Zion, the white rocks of White Cliffs Plateau have had the iron leached from them by erosion. Opposite: The three peaks that make up Zion's Patriarchs were named after one Methodist minister's favorite biblical patriarchs: Abraham, Isaac, and Jacob.

Above, left to right: *Due to the erosion that has sculpted the sandstone in just about every direction, the rock formations in the slick rock area of Zion appear to undulate with motion. A lone ponderosa pine clings to the top of a pillar of rust-stained sandstone.* Below: *Typical of the arches in this region, the rock of Zion's Blind Arch was undermined by erosion, creating a natural arch and a symbol of great strength.*

Zion's Checkerboard Mesa is one of the strangest examples of erosion. The horizontal lines follow the beds of ancient sand dunes while the vertical lines are simply the result of cracking. Below: Sandstone pillars are silhouetted against a sheer wall of stone in Zion National Park. Following pages, left: One of Zion's most famous monoliths is the Great White Throne whose white and gray rock provides a dramatic contrast to the surrounding red rock. Right: According to Native American legend, a new day begins when the morning sun hits the peak of Zion's Mountain of the Sun.

Above, left to right: *The awesome rock formations in Zion are the park's biggest attraction, but its plant life is also interesting due to the scarcity of water and harsh conditions in which they grow. A delicate waterfall provides moisture for a variety of plants that flourish nearby.* Below: *Zion's Temple of Sinawava, named in honor of a Native American wolf god, is a deep canyon filled with still more fascinating rock formations.* Opposite: *The Watchman stands approximately 2,600 feet above the south entrance to Zion National Park. The Virgin River runs nearby and is one of the main forces of erosion in the park.*

Without a doubt, the national parks of Arizona and Utah have the landscape to feed the imagination. Whether it is the rugged, red rock or the desert wilderness, visitors are bound to be taken in by their beauty. As scientists and environmentalists continue to study the earth's past and fight for its future, they warn about the volume of people and vehicles that tour these parks each year—and about the pollution and destruction that occurs when these fragile environments become overcrowded. Traveling their many miles, from canyon, to cavern, to cliff, reminds us just how powerful, yet ecologically delicate, nature is—and how absolutely priceless.

The eroded clay mounds in the Blue Mesa region of Arizona's Petrified Forest National Park are strange moonscape-like formations.

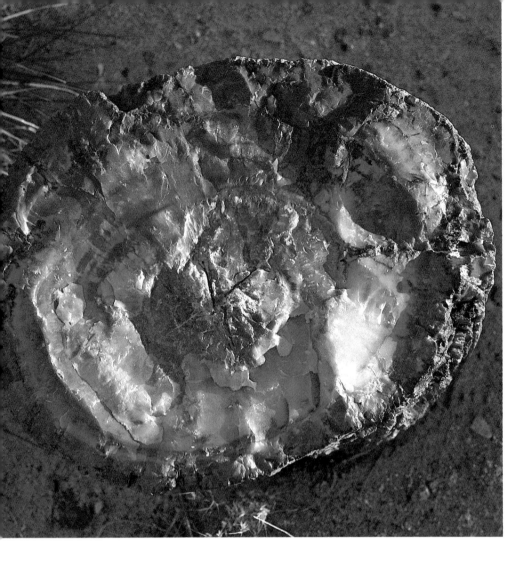

This page: *Crystallized cellular structures of once living trees have been preserved as petrified wood in the Rainbow Forest area of the Petrified Forest.* Below: *Agate House was a Native American pueblo built of petrified wood between* A.D. *1050 and 1300.* Opposite: *A pedestal log in Blue Mesa was once part of a petrified tree that cracked and broke when the earth shifted, lifting the giant tree above the mud, sand, and volcanic ash in which it had long been buried.* Overleaf: *Resembling a man-made bridge, these petrified logs are naturally connected by fibers preserved in agate and quartz.*

Index of Photography

All photographs courtesy of The Image Bank except where indicated *.